The Caribbean
A Painter's Paradise

WILLIAM WOOD

for Edna

MACMILLAN CARIBBEAN

'Tis blazing noon, fierce, unrelenting noon!
Pale Phoebus from the pinnacle of heaven,
O'er panting labor beats – the dark Maroon
To the cool woods, or fishing stream is driven; –
Fair damsels to Siesta now are given –
Noon's twanging signal hark! the welcome shell
Delights all those who in the sun have striven,
And frees them quickly by its magic spell,
  To bathe in crystal pool, or doze in shady dell.

WILLIAM HOSACK   *The Isle of Streams, or, The Jamaica Hermit*

Waterfall

I love the sea
when it's like this.
When you see is like this?
I love the sea.
Yeah.

Man,
that sea, man,
is full of my tears eh!
Yeah.
Full of my tears man.
I mean,
you know what
memories
that does bring back man?
You know how much
memories that does bring back?

CHRISTOPHER LAIRD   *The Sea at Evening*

Pelican Beach

When frequent Rains, and gentle Show'rs descend,
To chear the Earth, and Nature's self revive,
A second Paradise appears! the *Isle*
Thro'-out, one beauteous Garden seems; now Plants
Spring forth in all their Bloom; now Orange Groves
Diffuse their Sweets, and load each passing Gale
With heav'nly Fragrance; the Citron too, now
Breathes its Hoard of rich Perfumes; while All,
Their various Odours join, and to the Mind
Inspire a Likeness of what *Eden* was.

NATHANIEL WEEKES *From Barbados*

Estate House

Still sparkles here the glory of the west,
Shews his crowned head, and bares his jewelled breast,
In whose bright plumes the richest colours live,
Whose dazzling hues no mimic art can give –
The purple amethyst, the emerald's green,
Contrasted, mingle with the ruby's sheen;
While over all a tissue is put on
Of golden gauze, by fairy fingers spun –
Small as a beetle, as an eagle brave,
In purest ether he delights to lave;
The sweetest flowers alone descends to woo,
Rifles their sweets, and lives on honey-dew –
So light his kisses, not a leaf is stirred
By the bold, happy, amorous humming-bird;

M J CHAPMAN   *From Barbadoes*

Humming Bird Beach

Love for an island is the sternest passion:
pulsing beyond the blood through roots and loam
it overflows the boundary of bedrooms
and courses past the fragile walls of home.

PHYLLIS ALLFREY   *Love for an Island*

Sunday Morning

I remember back home
Sky blue
Sea clean
Sun warm and radiant,
Looking at himself in the water,
Glittering and shining in the morning waves.

We stripped to the waist
Cleaned the deck of a tired old tub
Getting ready to sail.
We scrubbed, cleaned, washed, fixed –
But my cousin had forgotten the engine didn't work –
No sailing today.

DONALD PETERS   *I Remember Back Home*

Fishing Boat Harbour

Broad sun-stoned beaches.

White heat.
A green river.

A bridge,
scorched yellow palms

from the summer-sleeping house
drowsing through August.

Days I have held,
days I have lost,

days that outgrow, like daughters,
my harbouring arms.

DEREK WALCOTT *Midsummer, Tobago*

The River

Uncle Time is a ole, ole man . . .
All year long 'im wash 'im foot in de sea,
long, lazy years on de wet san'
an' shake de coconut tree dem
quiet-like wid 'im sea-win' laughter,
scraping away de lan' . . .

DENNIS SCOTT   *Uncle Time*

Pelican

Fruit in a bowl.

Full goldenapples with veined skins so fine
That just to look might burst them –

                                               tangerines
For all the world like small green solid bells
Promising little kisses of astringency.

Yellow bananas, cool and firm to feel
Lying in curves of silken-tongued delight.

And great plumpted mangoes, sweetness to the seed.

Huge cut pawpaws bearing dark-seedling cargoes.

And sapodillas with their sweet, brown kernels
Aching to change to sugar once again.

Tropical fruit.

A J SEYMOUR *Fruit in a Bowl*

Fruit and Flowers

This island is heaven – away from the dustblown blood of cities;
See the curve of bay, watch the straggling flower, pretty is
The wing'd sound of trees, the sparse-powdered sky, when lit is
The night. For beauty has surrounded
Its black children, and freed them of homeless ditties.

DEREK WALCOTT   *As John to Patmos*

Wall Flower

Then the grasslands.
Muted green in a pallette of olive
Fading two tones lower to sienna
Than the rust-ochre blades aglint,
Crowning the coconuts
Lining the twisting road –
Incandescent ribbon
In open sunlight.

WILLI CHEN   *Country Days*

Hill House Landscape

The window in the little redwood gallery where I'd sit for hours
watching the canefields groan the blackbirds march across the
road
the sun swing downwards to the shakshak
tree the mulecarts creak/ing home . . .

EDWARD KANAU BRATHWAITE   *Indigone*

Carriage House

Girl chile darling yuh ole muddah hay
Praisin' de Lord fuh 'E blessing an 'E mercies
You is many many blessin's an' all o' me mercies
Glory to God!
Uh get de 5 pound note an' de Christmas card
God bless yuh!
But de carpenter ain' come to put on de shed-roof
So uh spen' it an uh sen' Rosy pretty to de
Exhibition gal, yuh should see she!

BRUCE ST JOHN *Letter to England*

Post Box

I can hear the gospel
of little feet
Go choiring
Down the dusty asphalt street

Beneath the vast
Cathedral of sky
With the sun for steeple
Evangeling with laughter
Go the shining ones
The little people.

ROGER MAIS *Growing Up*

St John's Cathedral

Let my roots go deep, go deep,
Seeking fabled streams
While the trade winds sound and sweep
Through my leafy dreams.

H A VAUGHAN *The Tree*

Flamboyant

A lizard sleeps upon the window-bar;
the window-curtains fold in sleep
their sleeping jungles of convolvulus.
The noonday sun lies shadowless
with all its gold upon the trees –
their reds upon the sky like pain.

GEOFFREY DRAYTON *Still Life*

Paw-Paw House

I shall return to loiter by the streams
That bathe the brown blades of the bending grasses,
And realize once more my thousand dreams
of waters surging down the mountain passes.

CLAUDE MCKAY   *I Shall Return*

Sugar Mill Pond

There was a roaring in the wind all night
The rain came heavily and fell in floods;
But now the sun is rising, calm and bright
The birds are singing in the distant woods.

WILLIAM WORDSWORTH *Resolution and Independence*

Dawn Pond

How calm how beautiful comes on
The stilly hour when storms are gone
When warring winds have died away
And clouds, beneath the glancing ray
Melt off, and leave the land and sea
Sleeping in bright tranquility . . .

THOMAS MOORE   *The Golden Hour*

Room with a View

I came to an opening where the country seemed to descend to the west, and a little spring of fresh water, which issued out of the side of the hill by me, ran the other way, that is, due east; and the country appeared so fresh, so green, and so flourishing that it looked like a garden.

DANIEL DEFOE *Robinson Crusoe*

Tropic Waterfall

In the swamp in secluded recesses
A shy and hidden bird is warbling a song.

WALT WHITMAN   *When Lilacs Last in the Doorway Bloomed*

Egret

I should like to rise and go
Where the golden apples grow;
Where below another sky
Parrot islands anchored lie.

ROBERT LOUIS STEVENSON *Travel*

Parrot Beach

Peace waits among the hills;
I have drunk peace,
Here, where the blue air fills
The great cup of the hills,
And fills with peace.

ARTHUR SYMONS *Montserrat*

Hill Village

Contents

The author and publishers wish to thank the following who have kindly granted permission to reproduce their poems:
Curtis Brown Group Ltd. on behalf of Phyllis Shand Allfrey for 'Love for an Island'. Joy Vaughan Brown for 'The Tree' by H.A. Vaughan. Willi Chen for 'Country Days'. Carl Cowl, Administrator of the Archives of Claude McKay, for 'I Shall Return' from *Selected Poems of Claude McKay*, published by Harcourt Brace Jovanovich (1981). Geoffrey Drayton for 'Still Life'. Faber & Faber Ltd. for 'Midsummer Tobago' and 'As John to Patmos' by Derek Walcott. Christopher Laird for 'The Sea at Evening'. Oxford University Press for four lines from 'Indigone' by Edward Kamau Brathwaite from his book *Sun Poem* (1982). Brian Read on behalf of the Literary Estate of Arthur Symons for 'Montserrat'. Elma Seymour for 'Fruit in a Bowl' by A.J. Seymour. Michael Sloly on behalf of the Estate of Jessica Taylor for 'Growing Up' by Roger Mais. University of Pittsburgh Press for 'Uncle Time' by Dennis Scott from his book *Uncle Time*. Copyright © 1973 by Dennis Scott.
Every effort has been made to trace all the copyright holders but if any have been inadvertently overlooked the publishers will be pleased to make the necessary arrangement at the first opportunity.

First published 1993

Published by THE MACMILLAN PRESS LTD
London and Basingstoke
Associated companies and representatives in Accra, Auckland, Delhi, Dublin, Gaborone, Hamburg, Harare, Hong Kong, Kuala Lumpur, Lagos, Manzini, Melbourne, Mexico City, Nairobi, New York, Singapore, Tokyo.

ISBN 0 – 333 – 59214 – X

Printed in Hong Kong

A catalogue record for this book is available from the British Library.

Front cover: *Waterfall*
Title page: *Shaded Beach*